# Strange Cargo

## Recent Titles from smith|doorstop

The Poetry Business publishes pamphlets and collections under the smith|doorstop imprint, children's poetry under the Small Donkey imprint and pamphlets from young poets as part of The New Poets List, as well as *The North* magazine. Recent and forthcoming publications include:

**Pamphlets:**
*The Laureate's Choice Collection 2016*: Geraldine Clarkson, Zeina Hashem Beck, Mark Pajak and Tom Sastry
Stephen Knight, *A Swansea Love Song*
Julie Mellor, *Out of the Weather* (July 2017)
Matt Black, *Spoon Rebellion* (July 2017)

**Anthologies:**
*CAST: The Poetry Business Book of New Contemporary Poets*
*The Sheffield Anthology*
*Thirty at Thirty: Celebrating 30 years of smith|doorstop pamphlets*

**Small Donkey:**
Carole Bromley, *Blast Off!*
Dean Parkin, *The Bubble Wrap* (September 2017)

**The New Poets List:**
Theophilus Kwek, *The First Five Storms*
Jenny Danes, *Gaps* (July 2017)
Phoebe Stuckes, *Gin & Tonic* (July 2017)

Order the above titles now from the shop at www.poetrybusiness.co.uk

# Strange Cargo

*Five Australian Poets*

Edited and Introduced by
**Paul Munden**

smith|doorstop

Published 2017 by
smith|doorstop
The Poetry Business
Bank Street Arts
32-40 Bank Street
Sheffield S1 2DS
www.poetrybusiness.co.uk

ISBN 978-1-912196-04-3

British Library Cataloguing-in-Publication Data.
A catalogue record for this book is available from the British Library.

Typeset by Tim Morris
Printed and bound by CPI Group (UK) Ltd, Croydon, CR0 4YY
Cover design by Tim Morris
Cover photo: Paul Munden

*Strange Cargo* has been published in partnership with the International Poetry
Studies Institute (IPSI), Faculty of Arts and Design, University of Canberra,
Australia. www.ipsi.org.au

**ipsi**

smith|doorstop Books is a member of Inpress, www.inpressbooks.co.uk.
Distributed by NBN International, Airport Business Centre, 10 Thornbury Road
Plymouth PL6 7PP

The Poetry Business gratefully acknowledges the support of Arts Council England.

Supported by
**ARTS COUNCIL**
**ENGLAND**

# Contents

Sarah Holland-Batt

# Introduction

In her poem, 'The Chest', Lucy Dougan conjures a haunting memory of a chest in the attic, in which 'childhood threats lay coiled':

> I should be sensible and never shut myself in,
> even though at times, believe me,
> I yearned to be strange cargo
> showing the whites of my eyes through openings,
> to wake at sea to jolting cold and foreign voices.

The child and the poet are as one, yet they are also multiple beings, inhabiting both inner and outer worlds, mercurial.

Poems show us strange things about the world; they take us to strange new places where we, readers, become 'strange cargo' ourselves. At the same time, ours are the 'foreign voices' to which the poems wake. In this anthology, published in England, a selection of work by five Australian poets is subject to all these shifting perspectives. Interestingly, all five have spent significant and productive time overseas: Jen Webb lived in South Africa, New Zealand and Canada before settling in Australia; Sarah Holland-Batt spent her childhood in both Australia and the US; Cassandra Atherton has been visiting scholar at Harvard and a fellow at Sophia University, Tokyo; Paul Hetherington wrote a recent book while undertaking an Australia Council for the Arts Literature Board Residency at the BR Whiting Studio in Rome; and Lucy Dougan, born in Perth on the western coast of Australia, to which she has returned, is seen in this volume writing with disarming clarity about experiences in Naples and London.

Notable here is the presence of the prose poem, a form enjoying considerable popularity in Australia, as indeed it is in the UK. One poet, Cassandra Atherton, writes exclusively in that form, weaving deft (and often very funny) intertextual references into her imaginative flights. For her, the prose poem is often an expansive poetic stage despite the relative brevity of the prose poem form. Jen Webb too prefers the fluid, often fragmented narrative that this form affords as her work explores the transformative nature of many 'ordinary' encounters and moments. Paul Hetherington has also adopted it for some of his poems, exploring within its frame the shifting and mysterious nature of the quotidian.

The compact nature of the prose poem contrasts with the quality of 'sprawl' that has been associated with Australian poetry, and there also is ample evidence here of that more expansive mode of expression. Both Paul Hetherington and

Lucy Dougan are expert at constructing poems that make purposeful use of free verse's flexibility. Sarah Holland-Batt is similarly skilled, her work often focusing with sustained, contemplative intensity on physical subjects. All of these works, in whatever form, take us into unexpected realms, where aspects of human experience common to distant parts of the globe are rendered with arresting, sensuous detail unique to their locale.

The five poets were brought together by the International Poetry Studies Institute (IPSI) based in the Faculty of Arts and Design at the University of Canberra, touring the UK in June/July 2017 for a series of conferences, poetry symposiums and associated readings. This anthology serves to commemorate the tour and introduce the poets – all well known on their home territory – to UK readers.

I should like to thank the major Australian publishers whose generous permission has enabled these poems to be shipped across the world: Giramondo, University of Queensland Press, and University of Western Australia Publishing. A number of smaller presses and publications are also acknowledged. Equal thanks are due to smith|doorstop for taking stock of the work and presenting it with typical care.

*– Paul Munden*

**Paul Munden** is Postdoctoral Research Fellow at the University of Canberra, where he is also Programme Manager for the International Poetry Studies Institute (IPSI). He is Director of the UK's National Association of Writers in Education (NAWE). Two of his collections are published by smith|doorstop: *Asterisk* (2011) and *Analogue/Digital* (2015). A new collection, *Chromatic*, will be published in Australia by UWAP in 2017.

# Lucy Dougan

Lucy Dougan's books include *Memory Shell* (5 Islands Press), *White Clay* (Giramondo), *Meanderthals* (Web del Sol), and *The Guardians* (Giramondo), which won the 2016 Western Australian Premier's Award for poetry. A past poetry editor of *HEAT* magazine and the current one for *Axon*, she works as Programme Director for the China-Australia Writing Centre at Curtin University and for the magazine *Westerly*.

## *The Old House*

> *Interiors are lost all the time* (Edward Hollis)

The dog ran in there.
It had been a mistake
to take his old trail.
He had picked up the scent
and bolted;
down the loved path,
through the painted green door
and down the black and white tiled hall
to the room that opened out magisterially to the river.
Her grandmother's house
that her mother had inherited –
she only understood
the sweetness of that later
– but it was not to be hers or her sister's
for there stood the strange man
in his ripped low slung jeans,
the beginnings of red hair
she did not want to see
snaking up his muscled belly.
He turned and smiled
as if he could read it all
in an instant;
a lanky girl and her dog
who had hightailed it home
or what had once been home.
She was not ready for this ruin.
She was not ready for these feelings
that came at once together.

That she wanted to hit him.
That she wanted to kiss him.
The light drained out of the river then
and all the childish games and dances
she had devised in that room
dived away like nymphs.
*You can stay a while you know*, he'd said.
But she was out and away with the dog,
pelting down the now foreign shape
of the path on which she had learned to crawl.

## The Chest

There is this attic memory for me,
a chest that stood at the bottom of the bed
and haunted us. A man made out of cloth rose from it:
spectral husband, killer, stained bride
or another self – unknown, uncountenanced.
All my childhood threats lay coiled in that chest,
ropes that led a snake dance down to other worlds.
I should not climb in or I will be found,
a blue child clad in rotting lace.
I should be sensible and never shut myself in,
even though at times, believe me,
I yearned to be strange cargo
showing the whites of eyes through openings,
to wake at sea to jolting cold and foreign voices.

Beyond the chest hung curtains patterned with an orchard
that cast a pied light made for wanderings.
I packed myself away with the stiff grace and sweat of tissue relics
and proclaimed – stowaway, chrysalis, cats for drowning
– that when I burst out I would not be me.
It was in this room that my father warned my mother not to stand
against the drapes for fear of calling up the types who slithered
on the smooth earth below or listed in clumps of rushes
further in the darkness by the river,
*barely human, don't think to call them so,*
and where my mother had told my sister and I about blood.
I hid in the chest after that and dreamt about this new dark river –
the force of how it ran and how to hide it.

This morning I stretched out of myself in bright winter light
and remembered the gift of a glory box from the father that I did not know.
Sturdy as a small coffin, it found me close to his own death.
What it should have held – voile for weddings, the sweet smell of
                                        swaddling clothes –
has been an empty ache to it. Oh life spun around me alright
with all its attendant wrappings but never so tenderly
as the word glory speaks – put on glory raiment like a king or queen,

those glowing souls of the ones who went before
and kept things shining and folded.
Or there is a word in his own tongue for glory box – *lettucio* – one to wake to
far off out at sea, borne away in a self unknown, uncountenanced –
which is a kind word that belongs to boundless days
in orchard light when all the room contracted to a chest.

Close it up then. But first or last just one more thing –
a man stands at the head of another open chest
and places his hand upon the heart, feels the solid pumping life of it,
a small fist that hits and hits again into his palm.
At season's change, the dark month, I lift the lid and curl inside,
my heart, peculiarly, opening out at this closing.

## Black Cardigan

While you are away
I sleep in your small black cardigan
with the diamante buttons,
the top one gone.
Little by little
I shed your glamour,
these sharp paste stars.
I am putting it on
and taking it off
in dreams where the ground
glitters with buttons and tears.

Lambs wool, it holds my breasts,
gives me back a waist, of sorts.
You've gone north, somewhere warm.
I'm heading south – snow
on the Stirlings
the weatherman predicts.
Days before we fronted the mirror,
sisters sharing glimpses
of wintered skin.
You said, here – take it,
I won't need it where I'm going.

## Sewing the Dog

This was the stitching that Ned helped her finish.
It was on holidays,
                    one of the last holidays
when the children still seemed children.
She had been moved by his eagerness.
*You see – it goes like this – take it through*
*on the diagonal and then to the next space behind –*
*yes – that's it – just like that.*
Appearing before their eyes was the running hound
with the French words around the pedestrian border
that would not be filled in
(perversely she liked this bit best)
and all the little clumps of flowers
through which the creature ran.
Months from now her brother-in-law
will bury the dog
they had all loved;
the dog the twin of this one
in the tapestry they are finishing.
It was French
like all good painted canvasses for stitching.
She found it in the throw-out bin
at the door in the craft shop
that had been on the corner for years
in which the people were unfriendly.
He would bury the dog
in just this pose
with her feet thrust out running
and, although not given to sentiment,
he would say
as he closed the earth over
*there – you will always be running*
but now,
          now
the woman and the boy
pull the wool through
and she runs her hands through his hair suddenly

and says *you're good at this*
*you could finish it*
*if you put your mind to it*

## The Forge

The women in these suburbs
flirt with the man who cuts keys, fixes heels.
They can't help being won over
by the light that glowers at his shop-front.
*Too sure of himself by half*
my mother would say.
He dyes his hair unflatteringly dark.
Once I took him shoes,
a second-hand pair.
*God, love*, he asked,
*what have you been doing in these?*
I laugh at the histories I could invent
for these strangers – sleep-walking, bacchic dance.
I laugh and say nothing
as he hands me the little green slip.
But I don't go back for a long, long time
(life more ruptured than the wreck
of shoes I handed him, impossible to unlock).
*Where you been darl?*
(if I could click my heels).
It's a story I cannot tell –
what kept me from redeeming
something fixed.
At night the women in these suburbs
unlock their doors
with keys fashioned
by the man at the kiosk.
They kick off their shoes
shiny and re-heeled.
They smile without quite knowing
how the man with the dark, dark hair
has eased his way into their smallest secret places,
snug in the palm, firm at the ankle.
And I chide myself gently
for not telling him the story of the book
I swapped for shoes
or why I had been away for so long.

## At Villa Bruno

At *Villa Bruno*
the presiding nymph
has black texta circles
around all her bits.
She watches us
with her nipples, her navel,
as we trail on opposite sides
of the long garden bed,
swapping names:
my bay for your *lauro*,
your *arancia* for my orange,
until our paths meet.
We fall into the spaciousness
of another century.
We might have trailing skirts, masks.
I take the crushed leaves, the proffered fruit,
and feel the blind nymph's
cool bemusement
as we step outside all drawn rings.
Nothing before
has tasted so close
to its wild estate.

## From the Queensway

No space is big enough for you
my thrift-shop Boadicea
with your Russian fringe.
You stride through tunnels,
past the posters of Hedda Gabler
with her eyebrows solidly
graffitied in.
On the tube
your hennaed hand
keeps time
to God knows what tunes.
*Get your own music* –
the old joke between us.
Next to you
the soulful boy
inclines his head
to listen in.
You hide your hand
so he can't read
your yin/yang moon/stars
but he alights whistling
anyway the gift you've given him
unawares.

## London, Misbooked

Up and up the stairs, dragging my load
to a narrow arrangement beneath leaded windows.
First, case in front of the bed
and then a kind of leap is what it took,
all of it unreal as the miles just flown.
Another leap off the end to the closet bathroom and
I was getting to know the cramped proportions
of old lives in this little eyrie.
I lay sprawled on the bed
like the pale skinned fraudster poet
only I was no marvellous boy
but reasonably along in life
with a full head of strangely curled hair
(perhaps our only likeness) after the drugs.
And I didn't die
but watched tele, something with Shirley Henderson in it,
filled out the breakfast order,
let the unaccustomed night fall on me.
Near sleep I thought this is probably the maid's room
but I didn't have to get up and do for anyone in the morning.
The doves came down to see me
and cooed their own flight histories
into my jetlagged limbs,
and if they were forgeries, too,
a human ear could not tell.

# Right Through Me

Little mortal,
afraid of all the sounds that
see into my body, afraid
of the techo's patient gaze
at the big screen where
*Mr Muerto* might be playing.
When they pin me to the plasma
the bony bit of me is tiny
with one perfect stone, is it,
or knot from some ancient accident?
*Can you remember any trauma?*
they ask, and I want to say
childhood falls from trees,
delirious, just because you could,
and being pulled roughly back
from dreaming on the Capri funicular.
But I just shrug
and feel the rightness
of withholding these lived jolts that
go right through me.

## The Brazier

There was something in it then, after all,
living like this,
driving and knitting,
and waking to biscuits and milk like a child;
reduced to standing in supermarket aisles
and reading the ingredients compulsively,
admiring all the packages
too much as she had.
Her father said it was a syndrome,
this love of packaging,
and she admitted tiredly
that all those years ago
he must have been, no was,
completely right.
She didn't have it as bad
as her cousins or her sister,
or it was not such a grand narrative,
but still she had it,
some form of homelessness
that she would end up
articulating or not.
Or she would just knit and drive and dip biscuits in milk
and read the packages from which the crumbs had come.
Night was best – the outdoor night,
sitting by the brazier
that had been an afterthought anniversary present.
The bougainvillea arched above, ghostly, most alive.
Were its flowers also leaves of a different colour?
They stood out in the blackness
as if husks of burnt paper had risen – unwritten scraps,
yet still substantial,
floating, not giving anything away.

## Dearest

The word dearest
opens the door
to another century
where a man might stoop
to adjust a woman's errant shawl.
And dearest in that time
begins letters, too,
that travelled distances in carriages
over fields in all weathers
to be received in agitation
or with calm
once their waxy seals were broken.
And even dearest blinking on the screen
sent snaking by hidden phone lines
can still contain this whole century,
the trailing shawl, the man and
the woman poised for this moment
of rearrangement and then,
forgetting us, they turn away.

## A Renovation (Girl's Work)

*I've always had a fascination with the needle... The magic power of the needle.*
*The needle is used to repair the damage.* – Louise Bourgeois

I have decided
that I will start mending
and that only my hands
will suffice.
I will, I know, get furious
with my limitations
but then there is something so
beautiful about the flawed work
human hands can do.
It will hold;
for think of a time
when only this labour
covered the body.
Can you imagine the tedium,
punctuated by the bright flairs
of the company of others,
the sheer graft of it, those calloused thumbs.
Also, an early memory of my mother's:
pointless work snatched from small hands
hot with a summer's day,
the teacher's voice admonishing
that this girl's work,
(*look at it!*)
is the worst
in the whole class.

## The Throne

In crisis
I go to the local library
and do not take out
the book I find,
*this one or that one first,*
*what matter?*
Outside beside my car
sits a strange chrome and vinyl seat,
part of a vanity set,
stranded, hieratic, ruined,
like the beautiful straight-backed
low seated chair-people
of Saint Martin d'Ardèche.
I do the visual maths.
Will it fit behind?
– no, there, rightfully, is the seat for our grandson –
I consign its odd allure to my phone's photo bank instead.
I sit on it only once,
open its cream frayed seat
with its tooled insignia of promise
*– nothing –*
What does it mean
for home to be a failure?
What does it mean
for other places to be a failure?
I leave the throne to its own
mise en scène, neither
desolate nor replete
were I to claim it.
There is, after all, no mirror
in front of which to place it
though I fix my hair and do my lips
before I reverse away.

## The Mask

This is the house of her childhood.
It's not standing anymore.
And in that house she slept
in a long thin room
in the bed for the youngest
against a bank of dimpled louvres
that broke up all the leaf shapes outside
so that they patterned
the patch of floor on which she played.

Below the place she slept
was a room beneath the house
and from that room
one summer
her mother had dragged out an old brown trunk.
Perhaps it held the other life of the house, she had said,
but to her child's eye its contents gave disappointment.

There were tatty papers
curling at the edges,
things that someone had begun to knit
and given up on.
Beneath this tangle something lay
that her mother snatched up quickly.
It was a face made of linen.
There were eye-holes, and a mouth
and they took turns in it
running crazily about the garden.
But she already hated it,
had relinquished it to the grass
where it lay, she imagined, sulking.

Breathless, she asked who made it.

*Probably my nanna*, said her mother.

*Oh*, was all she managed to say back.

That night she wondered
if there were more rooms
beneath the room under her bed.
How deep did they go down;
and if each of her mother's mothers
stretching right back
had left a fearful face there
for her to try on?

# Cassandra Atherton

Cassandra Atherton was a Visiting Scholar in English at Harvard University in 2016 and a Visiting Fellow in Literature at Sophia University, Tokyo, in 2014. She has published seventeen critical and creative books and has been invited to edit six special editions of leading journals. Cassandra has been a successful recipient of more than fifteen national and international research grants for poetry, including a Creative Victoria grant and an Australia Council grant. Her most recent books of prose poetry are *Exhumed* (Grand Parade, 2015), *Trace* (Finlay Lloyd, 2015), *Pikadon: Post-atomic Alice* (Mountains Brown Press, forthcoming) and she is the editor of the Spineless Wonders anthology of microliterature, *Landmarks* (2017). Cassandra was invited to judge the Victorian Premier's Prize for Poetry (2014, 2015) and the Lord Mayor's Prize for Poetry (2016, 2017). She is the poetry editor of *Westerly* magazine.

## *P.R.B.*

I wish I had been painted by Millais. Maybe not as Ophelia in a tepid bath. Perhaps as Lady Macbeth. Or Titania. Or Portia. I used to make you sit on a little wooden stool and pretend you were painting me. Stroke after stroke rasping against the canvas. I would unravel my strawberry plaits and stare at you. Sherry eyes. Corsage at my neck. Picking up the small crumbs of wedding cake and passing them through my gold ring. Nine times. But you still didn't get the hint. And so I am suspended in that moment. Forever bridesmaid. I can't be Effie to your Ruskin. So blot out the canvas with grey. Euphemia's hagiography turns on a wheel and a bear, but I can't be your martyr. Writhing in my skin, I call out to Rossetti to paint me. I make you call me Guggums and cling to wild heartsease. We both know the laudanum comes later. So you paint me. *Regina Cordium*. Hooded lids. Heart shaped pendant. There are two still babies in the shadows. One within and one without. Broken hearted, I become your posthumous Beatrice. Dig me up Dante! Exhume me. Consume me. Shift the soil between us and gather me in your arms. Chase your journal of poems around my coffin with your fingertips as you hold me. Let me hear your mew of pleasure when you have it. At last. My copper hair fills the empty space. But the worm's hole in your journal eats away at your heart.

# Stella

Last night I pressed my body to the cold tiles on the bathroom floor. Face down. Recumbent. Prone. To making mistakes. My torso left a hot patch beneath the vanity basin. When you came to find me I had misted up the mirror with my heat. I shifted sideways to find fresh tiles while you wrote the words 'We've had this date with one another from the beginning', on the steamy glass. You stepped into my hot spot. Toes curling into the warmth. 'Listen,' you said, 'can you hear it?' Somewhere in my imagination a streetcar still grinds its way down the Desire line. Even though we both know it has been retired. Retrenched. Put to sleep. And now you will have to rely on the bus to take you to your Elysian Field. I turned my head to the left and stared at the sock line circumnavigating your ankle. You shaved in the double 'e' of Tennessee and called me your Belle Reve. Tristes tropiques. Blanched, I peeled myself off the floor. Sticky sweat clung to the white tiles. You looked for a moment at my flushed belly before taking the bottle of eye drops and tipping back your head, cap in mouth. Gagged. Censored. Silenced. It's Post-Katrina in the Crescent City and I'm still waiting for more levees to burst. Me with my Hurricane box watching Treme on HBO. You drinking Hurricanes at Old Absinthe House in the Vieux Carré. Toulouse St. *La Blanchisseuse*. 'Don't worry,' you told me once, 'it's only a paper moon.' Both knowing it is only you who sails over the cardboard sea. I'm just papier-mâché. You chew me up and spit me out. Pulp. Palpitations. So I paste myself onto you. Moulding myself into your curves. But you're not waiting for the glue to dry. We rot from the inside out.

## Pineapple

Pineapple gives me atlas tongue. But I eat it and travel the world on my tastebuds: pineapple for breakfast in Hawaii with frangipanis and pink ahi poke. I never got to the Dole plantation, I was busy drinking Piña Coladas on the beach. There were bags of sweet pineapple rings by the side of the road on our way to Queensland – too many hours in the back seat of my grandfather's yellow Ford, sticky fingers winding down the window and my grandmother passing me tissues. Sweet and Sour Chicken in Hong Kong was tart and toffee coloured and stained the plate orange. A deconstructed pineapple upside-down cake on your birthday in New York was a disappointing sponge with candied pineapple on the side. You blew the candle out, I ate the sugary pineapple ring. In our apartment I made you the Betty Crocker recipe. You told me to close my eyes, lit a stumpy candle and said I could have your wish.

## Faulkner

My mother is a fish. I have buried her three times already, but the water table is high and she floats to the surface. I cleaned her, using scissors to cut through the bones attached to her pelvic fins, but I can't cross the river while her cloudy eyes are directed at the sky. The tackle box is full of the rusty hooks of untried catches. I take a pitted sinker and use the fishing line to weigh down her fleshy isthmus. There is water in my shoes but I can feel the stones rise beneath my feet.

# Eidolon

*After Kim So Yeon*

You overwrite the darkness; a ghosted image with two parallel overstrikes searching for a vanishing point. I have been here before; fairy lights dot the limbs of the persimmon tree. As the leaves fall, you suspend my noise with your smooth silences; a hibernation of longing forms on our breath. There is skin and bone between us, a currency of signs to be decoded when we part. I'm no semiotician, I can't expand time to fit between the wringing of your hands, but as the afternoon gives way to dusk, I read your stillness in the palm of my hand.

## Alice

I can't do this any more. Not even for you. Not even for the Happy Meal
you buy me after we have sex every Saturday afternoon. Do you know I only
eat the cookies? Do you know that I drop the fries down the drain in the
sink? One by one. Solitary. Loaning your copy of *The Waste Land* to anyone
who'll take it. You tell me to stick to Ovid. I tell you to try 'Prufrock' and
draft a new ending for us. You kiss me and still, behind your back, I drop each
fry down the sink. When you make love to me you watch your reflection
in my dilated pupils. And when you shower I rummage through your sock
drawer. Lone socks wait to curl themselves in their missing partner. I find
your Starbucks card and you read to me from *Moby Dick*. Always *Moby Dick*,
never *Pinocchio* or *Peter Pan*. I try to tell you that I prefer *Alice's Adventures
in Wonderland*. But you hush me. It is your silence. And who am I to break
it? I'm not anyone. I am occasionally Emily Dickinson. But the difference is
that I can dance on my toes. Life is 'full as opera'. I think about asking you but
it's late and my toes have gone to sleep between your ankles. In the viridian
night, I can almost believe you love me.

## Rapunzel

I called you Rapunzel
because you stole my hair.
Stole it from under my
sleeping head. Or from
the bathroom floor after
I was sick for you. I
could've danced in red
shoes with a plait striking
the curve of my back. If it
weren't for you. I could've
drunk champagne and
written letters to my
lovers. Poison pen. Poisson
distribution. I could've
been the nurse-child
grown up. I could've been
Kathryn de Merteuil. If it
weren't for you. Your father
left us when you guessed
his name. Guessed it just
to spite me. Sprite. And
now there is only us.
Bound like Chinese feet.
I could've danced en
pointe if it weren't for you
clinging to my knees.
Needy. Needling me.
I could've danced the
Tarantella if you had
let me out of the doll's
house to breathe. But
your greedy lips took what
Lady Macbeth despised.
Lactose intolerant. My
body rejected you two

months too early and I watched you die. In my head. Over and over. In the first eight weeks I flushed you down the S-bend but you clawed your way up and out of the bowl. My own foetal attraction. So now, what do you want from me? What more can you take from me? The colour from my cheeks on rainy days? The tannin from my grandmother's teacup? Tell me. What more can you steal from me while I sleep?

# White Noise

You outline the vein of biro between my toes with your tongue. Swirling around my second toe. Wormish. Nipping the tough skin on the ball of my foot, your ear pressing against my warm ankle. I think for a moment just how much I want you to take me ice skating. Just because I like the word 'rink'. Just so you can lace my white boots and hold my hand as I scream white puffs of air. Narnian Merry-go-round. But you will never take me ice skating. We only ever go to Smorgy's, The Ramada Inn or the Laundrette in Buckley Street – the one with the big tumble dryer for doonas. I initial your earlobe with my saliva. Nuzzling your carotid pulse with the tip of my nose. You tug on the ends of my hair, your pointy hip bones burrowing into me. Urging me to reach for my blue biro. I scrawl the first sentence of *Rebecca* on your back. You guess it's Du Maurier by the time I get to the capital 'M' for Manderley. You take the biro from me and press the nib into the freckled pits behind my knees. I ask you to press harder. Pleading with you to write your words in my plasma. Clear, sticky, cherry-tinted words. 'For a long time I used to go to bed early.' I smile. My skin singing. I want you to continue, to cover me in Proust. But you get impatient and paw at my thighs. I always preferred yo-yos to madeleines anyway so I snatch the pen from you and draw a stave down your backbone. Curly treble clef beneath your jutting shoulder blades. I colour in the crotchets but semibreves have always been my favourite. You guess it is *La Wally* from the fourth bar. And somehow you know it is connected to my desire for ice skating. Snow. Avalanche. Stalactites and stalagmites. Once you told me an obsession with white could only lead to sickness or marriage. And you said that neither of those were appealing. Neither of them could bind you to me. I search for my mohair beanie under the bed. The one with the big pom-pom my nana knitted for me. As I search, you brand me with the overture to 'Crazy for You' and I pretend I am a bass as you stroke my hips. For a moment you become the pointy stand that rests on the polished floorboards, supporting the bass. And then you are tired of games. So tired you refuse to list all the songs that have 'Lucy' in the title on the soles of my feet. I try to scrawl all the characters from John Fowles' oeuvre down your right arm but you are already packing the sheets into the laundry basket. You toss me my figure skating magazine while we dress. In silence. We leave the washing in the machine while we go to Smorgy's. Halfway through a bite of cheesy toast I blurt out, 'Nicholas Urfe'. You pick up your fork and scratch 'Sarah Woodruff' into my palm. Maybe tomorrow I will ask you to take me ice skating. Maybe tomorrow after you have written your blockbuster on my eyelids.

## Dot

I live in ellipses; between the spots that dot the page. Evenly spaced they hide our transgressions: the imprint of your fingers on my waist; the brush of your soft collar on my neck; my lips urging yours apart. At the end of the page they equivocate on the fullness of time. Some days the triad of circles conceal afternoons of champagne and concupiscence. Sometimes they point to your internal disquietude. You've thought about it one hundred times, a centenary of thought in a matter of weeks and you're back to where we started; with three stuttering dots ahead.

## Faulkner House Books, 624 Pirates Alley, New Orleans

We're on either side of large French doors. You're leaning against the buttermilk façade of the building watching the sky while I'm browsing the cramped bookshelves inside. I can see the edge of your ear, your elbow and your untied shoelace. I imagine you're looking down the walkway, thinking about Pierre Lafitte's escape from the Calaboose. On our first date you told me you needed space: an uninterrupted view of 'wanton stars and blue meadows'. So I slept on the very edge of your bed and left before sunrise. I move to the side hallway to choose a book of poetry from the two small armoires. I like the nook where my head rests just beneath your collarbone; the gap between your spectacles and your nose. I think of Faulkner in this front part of his house and imagine he liked to watch the moon descend across Jackson Square.

## L'heure Bleue

Blue twilight unfurls its splendour, a Didionesque gloaming for the lonely. I try to catch its tint in my cup, to taste its calm, but its inkiness spills over me until I am glass. Bathed in owl-light, I float on short blue wavelengths. I cannot be broken.

## *Not Published in LIFE. Hiroshima Streetcar, September, 1945*

In the charcoal aftermath, the Hiroden girls set their lands in order. Fisher Kings of the East, they survey their spectral landscape, a panorama of blasted earth and sterility. Scorched plains where the iron ribs of streetcars settle into the debris, they have said no trees or grass will grow for seventy years. Derailed by the shock, some hiroden are filled with whitened, swollen corpses. A hallmark of Beckettian mimesis, their poured-out lives gather dust.

## Kate Chopin's House, 1413 Louisiana Avenue, New Orleans

The pre-dawn hush is a votive offering as we stand looking up at the balcony's wrought iron lacework. Perhaps we don't love art or music in the same way, but we're both solitary walkers breathing in life under sleeping skies. I don't know if Degas ever met Chopin as they strolled down Esplanade Street and you don't understand why a woman has to have her pigeon-house, but New Orleans is a homecoming, of sorts, for both of us. Diverse and conflicted city, you see me in Degas' pastel, *Ballet Corps Member Fixing Her Hair* while I have only ever seen myself wading out into the Gulf of Mexico.

## X-Codes, or Katrina Crosses

You survive the flooding of the Lower Ninth Ward by taking cover in the bottom quadrant of my heart. Body count zero, I scrawl, to let people know you are safe. I'm your search squad, your protection against natural hazards, your libertarian. Next time the floodwall fails, you'll be waiting for me to save you from the wall of water. There will be room for you, for the seats pulled from the Louisiana Superdome, for mud-caked teddy bears, and even Fats Domino's flood-ruined baby grand piano. I collect brokenness in my left atrium. *Nature repairs her ravages – but not all.*

## St. Louis Cemetery, No. 1, Basin at St. Louis Street, New Orleans

In the Cities of the Dead, on the outskirts of the Vieux Carré, you squeeze my hand. I'm imagining being entombed, sealed in one of these above-ground vaults. We cannot return to the earth in a place below sea level, we'll drown. Here, the sun-bleached tombs hold long chambers and the dead are placed on the top shelves, turning to dust and bones in sub-tropical heat. I can't imagine being separated from you for a year and a day, placed in a holding tomb while we slowly bake in individual ovens. You reassure me that in the end, our bones and dust will share the same bag, tucked into the floor of our tomb. I see watermarks like fault lines from the floods on the vaults and imagine coffins set adrift by hurricanes. You put your arm around me. The living heart of us is bound tight with oak and pine.

# Paul Hetherington

Paul Hetherington has published eleven full-length collections of poetry, most recently *Burnt Umber* (UWAP, 2016) and *Gallery of Antique Art* (RWP, 2016). He won the 2014 Western Australian Premier's Book Awards (poetry), was commended in the 2016 Newcastle Poetry Prize, and shortlisted for the 2013 Montreal International Poetry Prize and the international 2016 Periplum Book Competition (UK). He was awarded one of two places on the 2012 Australian Poetry Tour of Ireland, and undertook an Australia Council for the Arts Literature Board Residency at the BR Whiting Studio in Rome in 2015-16. He edited the final three volumes of the National Library of Australia's authoritative four-volume edition of the diaries of the artist Donald Friend. He is Professor of Writing in the Faculty of Arts and Design at the University of Canberra, head of the International Poetry Studies Institute (IPSI) there, and a founding editor of the international online journal *Axon: Creative Explorations*.

## *Mustang*

We were children,
a whole mob of us
in Lime and Mission streets
near where the river turned,
when a blue Ford Mustang
careened off the highway
and fishtailed down Bell Road
into Caterpillar swamp.
The Council was going to pull it out
but it was nearly Christmas
and maybe the paperwork was lost
or someone went on holiday
because it mouldered,
half-buried in mud and water,
its number plates sunk
but its front bench seat
shining as if just polished.
We learnt the trick of casting logs and branches
across the mush of waterweed
and climb-walking our way
to an open side window, sliding in.
We'd watch the day become blank
in the stand of drowned trees
that a hundred years ago had been forest,
stowing magazines under seats,

making gauche declarations,
drinking sherry we'd filched from our parent's flagons
as candles guttered, scorching the vinyl.
One by one we moved away,
our families broken by divorce
or seeking a better district.
The Mustang remained: a carapace
rusted-through with recollection
of skinny, absurd children
standing on the bonnet
playing at pirates above floating weed,
growing towards what they would know
imperfectly.

# Chicken

Later, as we were being suspended from school,
we were instructed to consult our consciences –
'If you ever mean to return to this place...'
The dark hallway ran with outlandish rumours
of our expertise, who had disabled
the history teacher's scooter. Where the road
curved past the school he accelerated
straight into the lake among the ducks.
It hadn't been his bossy irritation
or the murder of his dull monotone –
these, and other crimes, we had forgiven.
It was what he did to noisy Amy (who
had Down syndrome and adored her chickens),
bringing a dead bantam into class,
hanging it from the ceiling: 'This a lesson
for girls who should not talk unless they're asked.'
When she ran from the classroom he had smirked
and written a lesson on the Boer War.
We liked Amy's cooing gentleness
and smile that forgave all we might do.
The next week, climbing from the lake,
his anger made him do a kind of jig
and Amy was there, hiding with handkerchief
stuffed in her mouth – our amazed accomplice.
Ever afterwards that bend in the road
was called *The Folly* by the students who
in this way remembered his transgression.

# Through a Window, Looking Back

At last, she thought, looking back
through the train's jiggling window,
seeing the Italian countryside
like a Giorgione landscape.
But what was this 'at last' –
it was hardly being here
away from family and domestic routine,
though, it's true, she'd longed for that;
for an absence of needing to be
what others required.
And it wasn't this sense of space,
the chance to do as she chose –
yes, she enjoyed it,
looking forward to the galleries
and canals of Venice – the dank smells
and superb gilded horses of San Marco.
No, this sensation was like vertigo
or the stomach dropping into space
on a steep climb –
thinking of the man she'd meet.
It would be ordinary enough
but it would be her own, entirely,
not possessed by children
or the years that had smoothed her marriage
so that even arguments
had lost their heft.
She remembered it –
how once they'd been at loggerheads
for two days, and on the third, had made love
and had barely known each other
or themselves. She'd wanted to keep that –
the not-knowing, the animal life
that had risen. She had wanted
to stay strange to herself.

## Fox

That day, in his yard,
herding cattle for drenching –
all that slop and kicked wet –
a bony fox trotted
away from the henhouse,
blood on its orange
like a gash in beauty.

He knew what he'd find
but dawdled in going,
hefting a spade,
twisting beans like clusters
of tangled sinkers
from triangulations
of tight, leaning pickets.

The hens were a mess
and he buried them quickly,
dispatching one
that was twitching and beaking,
shrugging anger
away from shoulders.

Later that day, as cattle fed,
he jumped the creek
where he often caught yabbies,
remembering hoisting
his wife and child
out of a flood,
joining young saplings
with a wrist-thick towrope.
The perished rope
was high in the canopy
and dark with lost seasons.

A woman he'd met
when buying horse blankets
had come for five weeks.
Every still evening
they'd watched grey teals
skim the low dam
and the wedge-shaped white
of their underwing.

In last week's post
he'd received a snapshot –
'something to keep
of that sweet holiday'
and 'sorry I won't
be seeing you soon' –
two of them smiling
at camera and tripod,
a fox behind them
crossing cleared ground.

## A Norse Greenlander, 1450

Ruminating,
she sharpens
her wieldy scythe.
Her woollen clothes
are close about her torso,
keeping at bay
the bleating, freezing wind
that blows across a stub of glacier.
Three winters now
her tilling has resulted
in frost-blackened harvests.
Her remaining sheep
are skeletons,
her children
are cramped with rickets,
her husband's ice-pale eyes
are shot through
with estuaries
of blood and forage.

## Squirrel

*for LD*

Each hair in the brush
is a thought in the squirrel;
each brushstroke a bound
into trees where nuts
are stored for winter.
Each deposit of paint
is a month or long year
when the squirrel has felt
the rain on its nose;
wind rattles leaves
and the storehouse of being
empties a little.
The painting thinks
with an animal's instinct;
wakes at night
with squirrel eyes;
searches long vistas
of grassland and forest,
sniffs at air
for what might arrive.

## Lorelei

Escaping from legend
she is becoming
slowly, strongly embodied –
sensing her blood's infusion,
through its copious networks,
feeling thighs tighten.
Her tongue tastes the season's
yeast and pollen, her nose
registers the tang of living water.
Nerves tingle towards sensation;
eyes open to water lily, reed
and earthy bank; and to the plunge
of birds; the glossy lineaments
of their water-skimming wings.
The thrust of her history –
jilted lover, water spirit, siren of the rock –
becomes a blur, like palpitations
in this unquiet stream,
and her old sense of falling
is now abstract – as is the agony
of high-sung yearning.
Loss still folds inside her
like a fleshly ripple; she is quiet,
knowing it cannot be undone.
Wrecked ships and sailors vanish
like hallucinations. The new year fills her
with keening relief – she'll no longer sing
a part in that old tragedy,
alone and content
in bird-haunted water,
feeling her body's shape,
mouthing her liquid name,
coming alive.

# Rooms
### for CA

**1.**

When you are in the desert and undulations of dunes slide toward you, you may remember a room. Under shiny stars, in the cold sweep of night, you'll hold that room close. And in blade-like morning, when light strikes the ground like scattered gemstones, you may stare at distance and know that room as if it were in your body – a place in which you're strong, no matter how small its dimensions. It is like a skin that knows the flow of your blood. It's where you discovered the value of limitation.

**2.**

Sometimes it contains a staircase; at other times it's small and spare, smelling of plum cake and tart cumquat liqueur spilled on linoleum. Occasionally it has ornate furniture and colourful half-pulled drapes. A boy hides behind a chest; a girl rubs a dress's green satin between fingers. A dog pants; a bath runs nearby. The girl stands on tiptoe, looking through a cobwebbed window. Later the boy sucks the inside of her thigh and she holds onto his hair. Sometimes the room is elongated, high in a building. There are dark floorboards; light squeezes through shutters.

**3.**

Rooms are informed by what's no longer there – light that wonders at you lying in a cot; space circling; dark drowning; walls like an unfixed firmament of mind. You grow up and forget those rooms but they cling; become stairs without end; an intimate boudoir of dreaming; a lit mystery behind doors – always old-fashioned, as if belonging to a different century. They are like early touch, haunting every exploration.

## What Was Left

A towel and bathing cap remained, and a tattered copy of a novel: *The Red Room*. They belonged to 13-year-old Lena, his Swiss pen pal, who stayed for five weeks during a ferocious summer. Nearly every day his parents took them all to the beach – his sisters, friends, the next-door-neighbour's kids – where they ate canned beans on balmy evenings. An uncle took them to a riverfront resort. They played table tennis and quoits, swam in a long blue pool. Twelve years old, he felt shy, while his sisters kept company with their dolls. Lena made friends with older boys. Twice his uncle brought her back to the resort – but negligently, as if enjoying her truancy. On the last night someone saw her in a dinghy near the falls. Rescued, half-undressed, she left the next day. His mother would not speak to his uncle. The novel lay for months in the spare bedroom like a remonstration.

## Parlourmaid

Death was a parlourmaid dusting the mantelpiece on which sat a clock, an ornate box, an unopened envelope. Her eyes possessed no feeling as she gathered and wound day like ribbons. Light left the room; furniture sat teeteringly upright, eaten by woodworm. 'I have done all I can,' she remarked before leaving. Feeble light returned slowly. Furniture creaked and settled. Love held nothing at bay.

## Wedding Dress

The old fabric began to come apart as she manoeuvred the dress carefully down her body. From the old photographs she was convinced that her size was right but lace came away and hemstitching pulled. Her mother had refused to wear it, preferring black slacks at a registry office. As a girl this had saddened her – to know the white dress had been there, handed down. She sucked in her stomach and the dress fitted. She stood in front of the mirror and imagined herself in the nineteenth century. Would that have been better – to be a possession; to be given away? She peeled fabric back over her head. Her grandmother had been escorted down the aisle by a father who later disowned her – something about propriety and family. The local paper reported her grandmother as resplendent. She stood in her underwear and thought, yes, a few alterations, phoning her best friend. 'Bring green dye,' she said. 'Bring pinking shears.'

## The Apartment

In that small apartment where a rusty fire escape clung to the kitchen's back like the descent of an arthritic trapeze artist, they cooked eggs and bacon and relished them unreasonably. They pushed late harvested asparagus spears into water to keep them fresh during the ticking heatwave as, outside, riots began, the city haloed in night light and anger. They walked the neighbourhood with trepidation chased by stares. When they made love it was usually against the damp bathroom wall while the cold tap dripped and their sense of themselves became vapour. After weeks they knew they'd leave their mutuality there. She handed him a note saying 'no way forward', dragging her suitcase. He inspected the rooms and found no history he could keep. She phoned twice, 'from Poland'. There were sirens backgrounding her voice as if a few streets away.

# Ghosts

You knew obdurate ghosts in that house, that your mother owned before you. Now it holds forty years of your own living, three marriages, boxes stacked tightly in a high attic. One day you found yourself fingering ten years of journals, like shadows gathered from old ground: 'I laughed at my seriousness.' Your life was laddered with words so you threw them away. A nebulous sea hefted light into wallpaper-brown rooms and ghosts stood next to the sideboard every afternoon. You spoke about your first husband who'd broken into the house and defaced your letters; and the second who'd left without warning, never to contact you again; then the third who'd died just as you were falling in love with him. Your paintings repeatedly represented him. Sometimes as we talked you addressed the empty air.

# River

There was never an explanation
as to why he walked into the river,
took hold of a log
and floated away.
They found letters
but the love he expressed
in sometimes obsessive detail
was no explanation –
except, the coroner declared
that perhaps it indicated
'a lack of a grasp', etc.
Someone who saw him pass by
said that he was waterlogged;
another said he sat upright,
as if triumphant, and was singing;
a third (unreliable) party
stated that he rolled and turned
and was having trouble breathing.
The coroner said that 'unless a body', etc.
And, certainly there was a report
that he had, after all, survived;
had walked out of the water
near a remote village.
'It sounds implausible,' the witness said,
who was rather bedraggled himself
with downcast eye,
'but he seemed to be smiling,
if shaking a little –
and appeared to be looking at something
not so far in the distance.
You know, like a thought
can sometimes hold a man.'

# Portrait of a Count
### for my father

Italians might say
this painting's an aristocrat
surveying his world.
But he also looks inward
toward his own death –
centuries ago
he was buried in Rome.
I try to connect
with his intimate gaze
as his dark velvet cloak
falls away from the frame
like a dying tide.
It might be my father
in a different era
(he always loved clothes),
sinking and settling
towards dark earth
as if soil is dragging
his gait to a grave.
The painting's tones
are astonishingly lifelike –
how those pigments have shone
through centuries –
yet now there's craquelure
dividing the flesh.
I see my father
living an afterlife
as a picture of someone
he never encountered –
and then he's suddenly
gone from the room.
Italians might say
he was never there;
that this is a Count
from old Roman times;

and I would believe them
except for the gaze
that quizzes me now
with my father's eyes.

# Jen Webb

Jen Webb works at the University of Canberra, and has been published in journals such as *Mascara Literary Review, Hecate, New England Review, The Amethyst Review* (Canada), *Bathtub Gin* (USA), *The Lake* (UK), and in translation, in *Poetry and Thought* (China). She has been anthologised, including in Page and Kelen's *The House is not Quiet and the World is not Calm* (Macau); Albiston and Brophy's *Prayers of a Secular World*; and Tredennick's *Australian Love Poems*, and her poems have been selected by Les Murray and John Tranter for *Best Australian Poems*. She has published six pamphlet collections, and is editor for the *Australian Book Review*'s 'States of Poetry' annual anthology; with Paul Hetherington, for the Mandarin/English collection *Open Windows: Contemporary Australian Poetry*; and with Kavita Nandan, for *Writing the Pacific*.

## Almost a Prayer

Beneath the crumpled skin, its muscles
flex and give: the sea, bearing down on the shore,
the swells high as houses. Young men play,
fly kites, build castles with the kids, while
women duckdive between the waves.

Beyond the surf a man swims laps – his bright
cap marks his path across the bay. Above him,
kites extol the sky. The girl in fishnet tights
swings a toddler high above the waves; swimmers play,
while waves break in earnest, dreaming of deep seas.

Boys buck and fly past on rusty bikes, beach towels
sway like prayer-flags on the lines, and all around
children set on mute play the night away. I am
almost home. I have drunk up the day and, washed
by the tide, I am almost undefiled.

## *Elegy*

What happens afterward is that you look, and keep looking. Something cold has burrowed under your skin. An emptiness. You find a pebble in your hand, but don't remember selecting it. Time lurches back, and like a fool balloon it spirals madly across the room. You will never see him again. You will look, and keep looking, but he has gone and taken with him all his stories, all his self, and all you can do is hold that pebble in your hand, hold it and breathe as the world shudders and then fires back into life, and steadies, and the passengers breathe more easily, and everything goes on as though nothing has happened at all.

## Driving Cross Country

An open road. Sun lights a folded world, and we are threading the needle, weaving between here and there. South of Tarcutta the road is scoured by flood. On our left, rape fields shatter, yellow, against the surface; on our right, trees shiver in waist deep water and around their waists, the mallee chokes. Birds are looking perplexed, testing out their landing pads. I stop the car and wade through scurf and mud-scum. Doing my bit. At the end, this is all the evidence there'll be against me: crows at a funeral, foxes crying in the night.

## At Hill End

For the first fortnight she drank only rainwater, drawing it from the tank, loving the satin texture on her tongue. The fifteenth day something swam to the surface of her glass and from then on, bore water was the only option. Gradually the taste of iron, a sandpaper flow, became her taste. The old tank dozed under its rambling rose, the hills and valleys of its corrugations becoming the domain of lizards and red backs, the subtle drip of its tap drawing snakes and roos to the back door, while the windmill turned, while from the kitchen window she watched the tank like she'd watched the disappearance of love.

## Table Mountain

The fire beating down behind you, the mountain burning, you run, a flock of panicked geese, calling out for comfort. The sky is lovely, oranges and reds, but no one's stopping to take pictures on a night like this. If you could, you'd pray. Finger puppets on someone else's hand. If you could, you'd imagine the great heavens opening up, wrapping you all in aluminium. All is crackle and pop, all is cough. You pause at the foot of the mountain, at the mouth of the bay, the patient frightened geese milling around like you. The smell of sweat, the smell of smoke. Coughing. Phosphorescent water, sleepy waves. Seagulls yawn and stretch, the sky opens up.

## Muizenberg Beach

The white sharks beyond the steel nets. The rows of candy-cane changing sheds where the walls are clammy and the floors are clammy and the smell is genteel decay. They are not hers, but she owns everything between. The hot gold sand, and the green water that in daylight breaks into lace at her feet, and at night becomes a shatter of light. The beach umbrellas canted at the right angle: they are hers too. And the ice cream men ringing their bells, and the children asking for coins. When she stands on the edge of the beach, and roars, even the sea loses its nerve.

## Painting the Room

It wasn't     till they came     calling that you
noticed the state of the place.     The walls
closing in,          the absence        of light
and on     the faded paint the stains of old
mistakes.     You know the          risks of
spill,          the marks of fire or of
tainted air. But you, you read the walls   and
not the rules.     Scrape it back and     damn
the dust.     It makes you ache but          faint
heart never won     et cetera. The stains
bleed     through your history          on the
unprimed wall: the shadow of last year and
how she turned     her head,        someone
called from          another room, that
difficult thing that you said.     Cover it
with colour.     The paint now     in your lungs
and on your hair.     Every word traced in
silk     white,        washed with easy coat
cream:     this is   what you wanted.   Now
you stand     inside the room,        the paint
got all over     your skin        and the marks
remain     like memory.     Wash the colour
from your skin.     It seems so simple    now it's
done,        the lines        drawn    in sand,
the troubled   nights,     it's     done.

## Family History

That house we bought when the children were babies. The one-acre garden you turned into yard. The midden out the back, filled with green glass and brown, 19th century baby bottles, logos we couldn't parse. I hauled it into the house, muddy bottles and old shards, while you furiously dug, you raged – *The mess! The waste!* – Relax, I said. It's just how they did things then. They had so little to discard. They dreamt no dreams of anthropologists, made no preparations for future judgments. You lifted a hen off your new dirt pile, and placed her gently down on the clean lawn. She strolled off, singing.

## The Loom

She has hauled out her loom, though she'd sworn she'd never touch it again. He brought her those skeins of mohair and silk, crimson and garnet and rose. She hauls out her loom, warps it up with torn linen and the ghosts of letters she never sent. Then it's the rush of shuttle, the clack of shed stick, the slow magic as images turn into form. He comes to the studio sometimes, but he can't make sense of what she is making. It's written in a language he doesn't know, a language of being left alone and then reclaimed; of fists against walls and nights without rest; of the body, and of blood.

## Bête à Chagrin

a thin morning, Canberra cold, and the cat
is sleeping outside, he's dozing out there
dying in the sun, not knowing it, he thinks
perhaps how sunlight feels on skin, how birds' wings
sound the air, he tastes the drugs on his tongue

this is the matter of his life
a life of feeling     not thinking. Of being     not might be
a human heart can't be: I am want, he is satisfied with *is*

for him an easy death, for me old words
like *chagrin* come to mind, and I
must make the call, rule the line

he purrs again, I stroke his staring coat
he's metaphor of course; all cats are, all loves
he blinks, dying in the sun

I can't find the gap between want and ought
now *might be* shifts into *will* and *don't* becomes *yes*
the sun the only bright spot on a hard-edged day

## What the Pumpkin Knows

What is it they say in Sierra Leone?
– There is nothing about the knife
that the pumpkin doesn't know.
Nothing about the knife
that the pumpkin
can't forget?

Every evening, so routine,
another small colloquial crime.
Another curfewed massacre.
And then the cleaning up.
The questions in the news;
and her eyes
on screen.

The journo asks,
*Which is worse: guns or planes?*

Her eyes
on screen. Not mine.
Not my son.
My house, my yard
not mine;
my son, not mine.

And what is it they say in Sierra Leone?
'For a funeral, any kind of crying will do.'

## Metamorphoses

Speaking of things that change – I am
older, greyer, more dense, but
the laurel bush, the white cow, the hind – these
forms escape me. Things no longer
change – or not in that way. Humans remain
disappointingly the same: legs, arms,
eyes, desires.
                    I too am disappointingly
the same. Till the light shifts in the living room,
the cat looks up from sleep, it's the shadow
of a god's descent, and branches sprout from my skin,
the snakes move in my hair, the swan between my thighs.
The urgent moment passes.

But outside the mysteries continue
to conspire – I can't tell where
the story ends and the world
begins – or vice versa – but they do
in their own ways start and end. Trees change
with flood or fire, Daphne blinks, sleepily,
from each leaf of her dark tree. The light portends.
The great swan beats his wings, and at the far side
of the field the white bull shakes his lowered head,
and the much more modern Cinderella
shakes the ashes from her shoe.

## The World Is Too Big

He died when I was away from home, not knowing it would happen, not expecting that something so momentous could arrive without its having made an appointment, but he did anyway die, and me without my thoughts straight without my face on without the words to say ready on my tongue. The world is too big in his absence, it takes a week to cross the street a month to make that call. It's too big and there's no space in it for all the words we failed to share.

## Walking with Nietzsche

He has been walking all day, and the mountain range has changed from brushstrokes on paper to something more formed. It will be days before he finds himself in among the foothills, or scrabbling up its slopes. One foot, then the other, and repeat. Time fills all the space there is, but he has time and space, and to spare. He has been watching the mountain now for weeks, and each step treads the image a little deeper into his skin. When at last he gets there, he will be mountain to the bone.

## Broken Things

I am learning, little by little, the craft of kintsugi: how to smelt metal, the right angle of pour, when to breathe on the wound as it sets. Call it 'gold joinery': no more stitches, no more glue. Fuck sutures: everything that matters will escape. Go slow: pour in the molten gold: fill every space. Yes it sounds a bit *you know*, but in the right hands. In your hands. I am learning, little by little, the art of wabi-sabi: how to find beauty in broken things.

## The Walnut Tree

The walnut tree gave up its richest crop in our last autumn there – the year the third baby was born, the year the blight arrived. Each morning I led the children through the little wooden gate to the orchard, and while the heavy dew stained our clothes, we gathered up the nuts, golf ball sized, still clad in the ball gown tatters of their husks. Each morning we ran back to the kitchen, shedding boots and coats, and held our fingers out to the flames. The nut pile grew. Some we roasted, some we cracked fresh, some we fed to the pigs. When you stepped barefoot on the shards of shells you banned them from the house. When you saw the litter of shells across the garden beds you had the tree cut down. The pigs were next to go, and then it was my turn.

## Huon Pine

It grew for centuries before he found it, sinking its feet into the cold southern soil, watching as the humans appeared, watching as the younger forests burned, and recovered, and burned again, as the seasons changed and the climate changed, as the protesters rigged hammocks in its limbs and as the loggers gave way. When it died, he hauled it down the rutted tracks, and carved it into boats and benches and guitars. He turned the last small block on the lathe. A golden bowl. He filled it with the shavings of itself. Sealed it with a metal grille. When he died, they took it to the dump. The tree is gone, and he is gone, and it is years since the shavings held their scent. I hold my face close to the grille, and breathe in what has no scent, a dead man's memory.

# Sarah Holland-Batt

Sarah Holland-Batt is an award-winning poet, editor, critic and academic. Educated at New York University and the University of Queensland, she is the recipient of a Sidney Myer Creative Fellowship, the W.G. Walker Memorial Fulbright Scholarship and residencies at Yaddo and MacDowell colonies in the United States, among other honours. Her most recent book, *The Hazards* (UQP, 2015) won the 2016 Prime Minister's Literary Award for Poetry, and was shortlisted in the New South Wales Premier's Literary Awards, the AFAL John Bray Memorial Prize, the Western Australian Premier's Book Awards, and the Queensland Literary Awards. Her poems have been widely published in journals such as *The New Yorker*, *Poetry*, and elsewhere, and have been translated into several languages; a Spanish translation of *The Hazards* is forthcoming from Vaso Roto in late 2017. She is the editor of *The Best Australian Poems 2017* (Black Inc), and Poetry Editor of *Island*. She lives in Brisbane, where she is a Senior Lecturer in Creative Writing at QUT.

## Approaching Paradise

Here in the white, white wing of a gull
you may glimpse paradise. In the flensing sun.
The prodigal sea, bent back on itself,
has the rough green mind of paradise.

Paradise is in the breadfruit's low sling,
the purple scrawl of bougainvillea up a wall.
It is in the yachts' clatter and wheel,
the fishermen's nylon stringing the wind.

You will find paradise in a whiting
drowning in a bucket of freshwater,
in the jammed blade of a fishscale
like quicklime under the thumb.

Women roast themselves in coconut oil
and children run bare-legged in paradise.
Praise them. And praise the black-faced bat
traveling even in sleep through paradise.

This fringe of stormstreaked shacks
with genuflecting surfers riding in,
this line of Norfolk pine. Wet dogs
nosing the muck of a king tide.

Praise the bloated body washed in,
the gentle nibbling of baitfish and bream,
bikini-clad tourists yanked out by rips,
the summer and violence of paradise.

A shark's slit corpse gapes pink on the jetty,
its head yanked on a hook like a sacrifice.
Its shank is smooth and black as paradise.
Men with knives kneel down like seraphim.

# The Severed Head

*photograph of Abdullah Sharrouf, 7, with a human head in Syria*

*I cannot take my eyes off that severed head.*
*Much as I want to, that is my symptom.*
                    – Julia Kristeva

He holds it clear of his chest,
outward, upward,
proffering. Five kilograms.

The weight of a hessian sack.
A watermelon hacked from the vine.
A medicine ball, raisin black.

His blue plastic Swatch gleams.
He is dressed for a school excursion:
checkered shorts, shoulder satchel,

shirt tucked in. He squints
from under his cap,
immobilised. Should he smile?

What would a smile mean?
The hair he grips with both hands,
dangles toward the light

the way you might lift a glass float
washed in on a king tide
by its neck of knotted rope

or a pigskin football
high before punting it skyward,
a lumpen prize. What praise

he receives is implied, takes place
after the iPhone's shutter
stutters closed and open,

before or after he knows
what he is holding, before or after
his father explains a heaven

as distant as Western Sydney
then sighs, a bus's slow exhalation
through idling suburbs,

the infidel moon on the rise.

## Thalassography

I have known these estuaries –
the channels and canals, the backwaters
that flush and eddy to the Pacific,

I have skimmed that muddied slurry,
felt the nip in the throat
where the salt in the air is the salt of the coast,

I have tacked where the tide is incomplete:
no rollers and breakers,
only an ebb that rocks the wayfarers –

a rush of silver, the gavel-smack of mullet
in the night, mud-crabs elbowing
denwards under concrete slabs of boatramps –

I have stalked where herons stilt and spear
baitfish in green afternoons,
cast crabpots in loose analemmas

to watch the black sonar spread,
tracked prawn trawlers on the broadwater
crawling back in the lavender dawn,

then sat at the jetty's edge
and shucked those tiger shells,
cast sucked heads back into the dark,

crushed mussel shell underfoot
for the burn of sharpened chitin,
stepped where stingrays wallow and idle,

shuffling their barbs, waiting to strike.
I have spent half my life in low tide –
nights where I have not known

if I am contracting or dragging out again,
where the movement of the water
is the movement of my mind –

unending comings and goings
of sounds and narrows, those entry points
to my two continents – and my history

is the history of currents: a canal small enough
to catch a childhood in its net,
water vast enough to divide a life.

# The Quattrocento as a Waltz

So long to the madonnas stiff as hairpins
and their blue capes like bells,
to the angels with Grecian cheekbones
and fishscale wings,
so long to our downturned faces
and halos bricking our heads with gold.
The inquisition of the light is over.
It was false, the teeth of an old woman in a jar.
It was unsteady, pouring in from everywhere.
It ruled our canvases with its endless directives
and its long, long gaze.
Here's a baby: he's an apparition.
Here's a god: he's a shank of meat.
Too celestial, too cruel.
Let the darkness shake out its bolt of silk.
Let it roam over us like a blind tongue.
Let it bury its razorblades in the citrons
and its hooks in the wild pheasants.
Open the window: outside is Italy.
A fat woman is arguing over artichokes,
someone is dying in a muddy corner,
there's a violin groaning in the street.

## The Pelican

Like the Memphis Queen she steams
downriver at pleasureboat speed,
the rolled umbrella of her beak
peony pink, wobbleboard gullet
dangling in fleshy bagpipe,
a flush of fresh shrimp
wooshed out of her rubber craw.
She stalks what she sees,
takes more than she needs,
the vast bayou of her appetite
swamping catfish shuffling
in mud, minnow churn, and the small
sweet cries of sausage dogs
on the shore – there is always more,
third helpings, the plate piled high
roadside diner style as she rides
stately as a motorcade,
dips her head in salute
along the antebellum scrollwork
of the shore, fossicks and prospects
with the rude gush of her influx
and pump, sucking shellfish
into gumbo, all swallow, all hallowed,
then with a swig of ipecac
upchucks the chum to her sons.
They struggle to keep up
as she steers south, singing hymnals
and cursing Union strongholds,
coasting to her holiday home,
a lavender estuary on Key West
where she wallows each year for a stretch.
Chiefly she goes to taunt the caimans,
sliding between them like a sly catamaran,
lobbying for a crackpot annex of Texas,
suspicious of the spoonbills' migrations,
always at war, muttering to herself,
still nursing her grievances about
the Louisiana Purchase
and the Pledge of Allegiance ...

## Decades

How you sit in a chair, for instance –
the way you lean back
so the legs crack and bow
like sea oat straining
to remember its shape –
that teetering could fill a decade.
Or your immoveable shoulderblades,
the muscle threshed there
in pucks and pebbles,
anxious knots it would take me
years to undo. Sometimes days
go as slow as decades. Sometimes
when we drive into the dangerous blue
of a snowblown afternoon
I watch your face and know
this is what is meant by an age –
late upstate sun hitting
the early silver in your beard,
grey cashmere rolled
back from your forehead
and the easy drift of your gaze
that makes me want to say
all the falling apart
will be worth it, even if
this is where disaster begins –
your pulse thrumming beside my wrist,
the mistake of having said even this.

# The Art of Disappearing

The moon that broke on the fencepost will not hold.
Desire will not hold. Memory will not hold.
The house you grew up in; its eaves; its attic will not hold.
The still lives and the Botticellis will not hold.
The white peaches in the bowl will not hold.
Something is always about to happen.
You get married, you change your name,
and the sun you wore like a scarf on your wrist has vanished.
It is an art, this ever more escaping grasp of things;
imperatives will not still it – no *stay* or *wait* or *keep*
to seize the disappeared and hold it clear, like pain.
So tell the car idling in the street to go on;
tell the skirmish of chesspieces to go on;
tell the scraps of paper, the lines to go on.
It is winter: that means the blossoms are gone,
that means the days are getting shorter.
And the dark water flows endlessly on.

## The Vulture

From his windblown roost, he leans out of himself
into morning, baggy shoulderblades swivelling
in a loose swoop, underbelly bulk
lagging in counterweight to wing,
each stroke ratcheting him into the clear levels of sky.
A reptilian meanness in the face:
raw pink skin rolled on the skull
in slack waves, the whistle flare of nostrils
like a shell's hollows, bubbled tar eye.
By some error, his flawed throat
makes nightmare music: a feline hiss,
the monstrous grunt of sex, all of it hatched
by a mind without pitch.
Brought keeling down to perch
at the swell of rot and bloat
rushing through that tunnelled nose,
he drops foot-first into jungle leaf
and when the jaguar pads away in blood,
stoops to feed. Shaman of transfiguration,
high priest of the day's death march,
he is the afterlife of all things:
child, star, pig, the small circumscribed lives
of the apes and fleas. Attendant, absorbed,
he snips the body from its shadow
with a surgeon's concentration,
sword-swallows tripe rosette,
trotter and gizzard to the hilt,
unzips sun-marinated gristle from skin
with scalpel cut and claw.
His eye flowers darkly.
Self into self without summit,
he gorges in silence, strops his beak,
then hoists out of the corpse on awkward wings,
veering up into the wind's periphery
as if returning from a foreign country,
diving straight into turbulence.

## The Orchid House

Pegged under banana trees,
our backyard hothouse was fixed summer
that boiled all year, a green humpy
breathing gauze in meshy sheets.
Indoors it poured artificial rain.

Under that striped sunlight
I crept the spider-heavy shelves
where exotics festered in their Latin names.
I torqued the twist-wires tight
around each trumpeting neck,
chivvied longlegs from potted dark
as outside the clouds blew back like years.

My grandfather spoke a strange pidgin in there,
knew Cat's Face from Queen of Sheba,
Snake Flower, Soldier's Crest, Sulphur Tail.
A decade late, I found a wrinkled block of newsprint
under the orange crucifix,
six men waist-deep in the Mekong
where the war's end could never come.

Death never reached those suburbs, not really.
Bodies in their Sunday Best
never lay on our cool kitchen table
stiff as celluloid dolls,
and last goodbyes
were told by nurses in chemical code.

When Grandad died, the wonky shack
grew wild, and creepers curtained over.
Through walls thin and threadbare
I heard them hissing, the cold wet tendrils
which could strangle, and grew on air:
teatree, tangle root, tongue.

# Manus Green Tree Snail

*A little boy was frying some snails in a pan. When he heard
them crackle in the oil he said: 'Silly creatures, your houses are
burning around you, and you sing.'*

        – The Medici Aesop

Here is nowhere.
Green cone inching up the branch
like a sail, cursed by its home.
White lip, yellow ring
spiralling up a leafing turban,
its body a foot chugging
over craquelure of lichen,
tugging its house,
trying to get rid of it
but glued there, hitched.
Everywhere the vagrant cries
of yellow-bibbed fruit doves
and imperial pigeons,
the scruffling of scrubfowl
under Saratanga trees, and the snail
still stuck, coming to its end,
slow as cement. High
in the canopy, the steady hack
of a trafficker's axe,
the thrash of fallen forest
collateral in the hunt
for the peashoot twist
of shell, each discovery
another knick-knack
to hang around a neck
or park on a mantelpiece
somewhere overseas,
one of those civilised countries
that only knows
how to love a thing
to extinction.

# The Hazards

How calm, how sudden the strait was that day –
humpbacked rocks sloping down into the sea
like the end of a long argument,
everything now peaceful again, but tiptoeing,
and past the sweep of gravelly beach
huge pink ledges lopped off in the water like bread-ends,
here and there a stump – call them islands – breaching at elbow angles,
and the slumbering bergs underneath, snub-nosed as marble.
At our feet, digger birds with shiv faces
cracked limpets solemnly for meat, blacksmithing,
and further out, specks of white seabirds fishing the whitecaps,
then that awful calm clear green all the way to the Antarctic.
Everything tasted of the sea, was of the sea.
You thrashed out first, hard, with your varsity calves
towards a far granite cheek,
the tiger's stretch of your body
powerful but ungainly, your torso turning
from side to side like something the ocean was rejecting,
and in a wild kick, a leaping up,
I saw you as a stranger might see you then,
your head straining above the surface
like a diligent retriever's, your eyes fixed ahead
as though the future were an island
you needed to reach without me,
and I knew I would never unlearn love like this, as distance:
your mild Midwestern college cut
dark and unstable on the horizon,
your too-white boxer's shoulders finite and ungiving
as you climbed the scrambling side –
*you* who would live if I died, *you* who were not I –
and I felt the shock, the parry
of my heart's start and stop: my life, my life.

# Acknowledgments

Many of these poems have been previously published in individual collections, anthologies, and journals, as follows:

**Individual collections:** Cassandra Atherton, *Trace* (Finlay Lloyd Publishing, 2015); Cassandra Atherton (with Alyson Miller and Phil Day), *Pikadon: Post-atomic Alice,* (Mountains Brown Publishing, 2017); Lucy Dougan, *White Clay* (Giramondo, 2008); Lucy Dougan, *The Guardians* (Giramondo, 2015); Paul Hetherington, *Six Different Windows* (University of Western Australia Publishing, 2013); Paul Hetherington, *Burnt Umber* (University of Western Australia Publishing, 2016); Sarah Holland-Batt, *Aria* (University of Queensland Press, 2008); Sarah Holland-Batt, *The Hazards* (University of Queensland Press, 2015); Jen Webb, *Metal* (Authorised Theft, 2016).

**Anthologies:** *AP Anthology 4*, ed. S. Holland-Batt and B. Emery (Australian Poetry, 2015); *The Best Australian Poems 2004*, ed. L. Murray (Black Inc, 2004); *The Best Australian Poems 2013*, ed. L. Gorton (Black Inc, 2013); *Cities: Ten Cities, Ten Poets*, ed. P. Hetherington and S. Strange (Recent Work Press, 2017); *Open Windows: Contemporary Australian Poetry*, ed. P. Hetherington and J. Webb (2016); *Prayers of a Secular World*, ed. J. Albiston and K. Brophy (Inkerman & Blunt, 2015); *Tremble: The University of Canberra Vice-Chancellor's International Poetry Prize Anthology 2016*; *Writing to the Edge: Prose Poems and Microfiction*, ed. L. Godfrey and A.J. Smith (Spineless Wonders, 2014).

**Journals:** *Antic Journal; Cordite Poetry Review; Mascara Literary Review; New Orleans Review; New Writing; Otoliths: A Magazine of Many e-Things; Overland Journal; Poetry; Poetry New Zealand; Rabbit; Stoneboat Literary Journal.*

**Exhibitions:** *Making Worlds* (Edith Gallery, Whanganui NZ, 2011).